Circus Tricks

written by Anne Giulieri

photography by Ned Meldrum

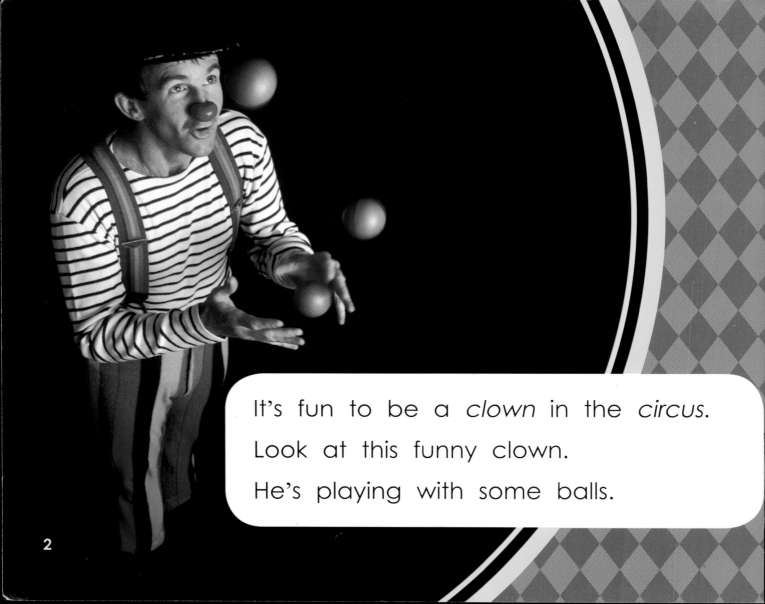

It's fun to be a *clown* in the *circus*.

Look at this funny clown.

He's playing with some balls.

We are going to be funny clowns today.

We are going to do some clown tricks.

It will be lots of fun!

At the circus, clowns can go along a *tight-rope*.

You can try this, too.

But **your** tight-rope will be on the *ground*!

You need to get a *rope* and a *beanbag*.

Put the rope down on the ground.
You can make the rope *straight*,
or you can make it *wiggly*.

Put the beanbag on your *head*.
Now put your *hands* out from your *body.*

Try to walk very slowly along the rope.
Your head will need to be very still,
so that the beanbag stays on top.

Can you walk along the rope?

Try not to fall off!

You can also try this trick with a ball.
This makes it very, very tricky to do!

Here is a circus trick with a *hula hoop*.
Put the hula hoop up like this.

You can try to jump in and out of the hula hoop.

A clown does this at the circus.

Look at this circus dog.

It's jumping in and out of the hula hoop!

You can try this, too.
It's lots of fun.

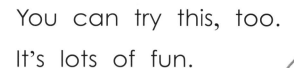

Now you can see that it's
lots of fun to be a circus clown.

Picture Glossary

beanbag

ground

rope

body

hands

straight

circus

head

tight-rope

clown

hula hoop

wiggly